Exploring Habitats

TEMPERATE FOREST
Habitats

By **Barbara Taylor**

GARETH**STEVENS**
GS
PUBLISHING
A Member of the WRC Media Family of Companies

Please visit our web site at: www.garethstevens.com
For a free color catalog describing Gareth Stevens Publishing's
list of high-quality books and multimedia programs,
call 1-800-542-2595 or 1-800-387-3178 (Canada).
Gareth Stevens Publishing's fax: (414) 332-3567.

Library of Congress Cataloging-in-Publication Data

Taylor, Barbara, 1954-
  Temperate forest habitats / Barbara Taylor. – North American ed.
      p. cm. — (Exploring habitats)
  Includes bibliographical references and index.
  ISBN-10: 0-8368-7257-6 – ISBN-13: 978-0-8368-7257-6 (lib. bdg.)
  1. Forests and forestry—Juvenile literature. I. Title. II. Series.
QH86.T397   2007
578.73—dc22   2006044329

This North American edition first published in 2007 by
Gareth Stevens Publishing
A Member of the WRC Media Family of Companies
330 West Olive Street, Suite 100
Milwaukee, WI 53212 USA

This U.S. edition copyright © 2007 by Gareth Stevens, Inc. Original
edition copyright © 2002 by ticktock Entertainment Ltd. First published
in Great Britain in 1999 by ticktock Publishing Ltd., Unit 2, Orchard
Business Centre, North Farm Road, Tunbridge Wells, Kent, TN2 3XF.

Gareth Stevens editor: Richard Hantula
Gareth Stevens designer: Charlie Dahl
Gareth Stevens managing editor: Mark J. Sachner
Gareth Stevens art direction: Tammy West
Gareth Stevens production: Jessica Morris

Picture Credits: t=top, b=bottom, c=centre, l=left, r=right, OFC=outside
front cover, OBC=outside back cover, IFC=inside front cover

Image Bank; 22c. Oxford Scientific Films; 2/3ct, 3tr, 3br, 4br, 5cb, 7tl, 7cr,
8/9cb, 9tr, 9cr, 10ct, 11br, 12tl, 12/13c, 13b, 14tl, 14bl, 14/15c, 17c, 17tl,
18cb, 18/19c, 19r, 19tl, 19bl, 20l, 20/21, 21c, 21tr, 21bl, 22tl, 22/23b, 23t,
24b, 24tl, 25c, 26c, 26bl, 27tr, 29tr, 30c, 30/31ct. Planet Earth Pictures;
OFC (main pic). Still Pictures; 11tr. Tony Stone; OFC (inset), OBCtr & bl,
IFC & 4tl, 32 & 6/7b, 2l, 23/cb, 4br, 5cr, 5tl, 6tl, 6/7c, 6/7b, 8l, 9tl, 10l,
10/11ct, 10/11cb, 12r, 13t, 15tl 15br, 15bl, 16bl, 16/17c, 17cb, 18l & (inset),
23r, 25tr, 25b, 26/27ct, 28tl, 28bl, 28/29, 29cr, 30l, 30/31lc, 31br.

Every effort has been made to trace the copyright holders and we
apologize in advance for any unintentional omissions. We would be
pleased to insert the appropriate acknowledgement in any subsequent
edition of this publication.

Printed in the United States of America

1 2 3 4 5 6 7 8 9 10 09 08 07 06

CONTENTS

IN THE WILD WOODS

Looking up from the forest floor
to the treetops, you may see only
leaves blowing in the wind. But
the world's temperate forests
provide shelter and food for a
huge variety of birds, mammals,
and other creatures.

THE LIVING FOREST

Mysterious and beautiful places, forests grow in nearly all major parts of the world outside the polar regions. Some lie in the hot tropics. This book is about forests in areas with a more moderate climate – areas located primarily in the Earth's temperate zones, which lie north and south of the tropics. Such forests occur mainly in the northern hemisphere, where they include the cold "boreal" forests of the far north, featuring predominantly coniferous (cone-bearing) trees, and warmer forests farther south, where deciduous trees (which lose their leaves for part of the year) are commonly found. All these forests are dominated by the seasons. They thus are very different from tropical rain forests, where it is hot and wet year-round with plenty of food available. In forests outside the tropics, plants and animals have to survive constant changes in the weather, including a cold winter season in many areas. The trees in these forests may provide food and shelter for a wide variety of birds, mammals, insects, and other creatures. Many plants and fungi thrive in rich forest soils. Yet huge areas of these forests, particularly deciduous forests, have been destroyed for their timber or to make way for farms, industry, and cities.

FOREST TYPES

Two main types of forest in the temperate zones are dark, cold coniferous forest, and warmer, lighter deciduous forest. Mixed forests also occur (*left*). Deciduous trees shed their leaves at the end of their growing season, carpeting the woodland floor with a pattern of russet, brown, gold, and red. Most coniferous trees are evergreens – that is, they keep their leaves year-round – although they may drop some leaves throughout the year.

NESTING PLACES

From tree holes and branches to piles of leaves on the ground, forests are full of nesting places for birds. The wood warbler (*right*) builds its nest on the ground and lines it with grass to keep its eggs and chicks warm. Wood warblers migrate to temperate European forests in the spring to nest and feed, but fly to warmer African climates in the winter.

SEASONAL SLEEP

Like a few other forest animals, the rodents known as dormice (*left*) survive the cold winter months by hibernating. To save energy, their body processes slow down and their hearts beat less often. A hibernating dormouse lives off fat stored in its body during the autumn, when it eats as much as possible. At intervals it wakes up, is active for a few days, then goes back into hibernation. In mild winters a dormouse may wake up too often and lose too much energy.

AUSTRALIAN FORESTS

The honey possum (*right*) lives in the eucalyptus forests of southwest and southeast Australia. Eucalyptus trees and shrubs are a rich source of nectar and pollen for animals such as honey possums, parrots, and bats. As they feed, the plants are pollinated – which makes seeds develop. The honey possum's long, thin tongue is tipped with bristles for soaking up its food.

EXPERT CLIMBER

Many forest animals are experts at climbing, which helps them find food and places to nest, as well as escape from predators. Long, strong back legs and sharp claws enable squirrels (*left*) to climb trees quickly and easily. They can descend trees head first because their back feet turn outward at the ankle nearly 180 degrees. A bushy tail helps them keep their balance as they leap from branch to branch.

FORESTS OF THE WORLD

EUCALYPTUS FORESTS

The eucalyptus forests of southeast and southwest Australia provide a unique habitat for an unusual collection of wildlife found nowhere else in the world. The forest canopy, or upper level, is fairly open, allowing dappled sunlight to filter through to the ground. The climate is seasonal, with rain falling mainly in the winter months.

Temperate forests grow in areas with more than 10 inches (25 centimeters) of rain a year and an average temperature over 50° Fahrenheit (10° Celsius) in the warmest months. Coniferous forests grow in an almost continuous band – generally above a latitude of about 50° North – across the top of North America, Europe, and Asia. Temperatures are usually less than 32°F (0°C) for six months of the year, and the growing season for plants is only one to three months long. Rainfall tends to be about 10-20 inches (25-50 cm) annually. Deciduous forest regions, further south, have temperatures above 50°F (10°C) for six months, annual rainfall of more than 16 inches (40 cm), and a growing season of three-and-a-half to seven months. In the southern hemisphere, temperate forests may contain unique trees, such as the monkey puzzle forests of Chile and the eucalyptus forests of Australia.

DECIDUOUS FORESTS

Among the trees often found in broad-leaved deciduous forests and woodlands (*left*) are oak, birch, ash, beech, and maple. To grow well, these trees need at least three times as many warm days as conifers do. In Europe, they grow mainly south of the Baltic Sea with a thin, easterly wedge tapering off into Russia. They also occur in eastern Asia – in a region running across China and Korea to Japan – and in the eastern United States.

CONIFEROUS FORESTS

The great coniferous forests (*right*) of the northern hemisphere make up the largest area of trees in the world. They are sometimes called boreal (from the Latin word for *north*) forests. From the Pacific coast of Alaska, they stretch eastward to the Atlantic coast of North America. They continue from Scandinavia to Siberia. In Siberia, coniferous forests grow as far north as 750 miles (1,200 km) above the Arctic Circle. From one end of Eurasia to the other, coniferous forests grow in a band some 6,200 miles (10,000 km) long and up to 1,200 miles (2,000 km) wide.

BAMBOO FORESTS

Bamboos (*left*) are giant fast-growing grasses with woody stems. They occur in forests in parts of China and Japan. Looking like tree trunks, the culms (hollow stems) often form a dense undergrowth that excludes other plants. The largest species of bamboo can grow as tall as 130 feet (40 meters). Most bamboos flower and produce seeds only after 12-120 years' growth, and then only once in a lifetime. This causes problems for animals, such as the giant panda, that rely on these forests for food and shelter.

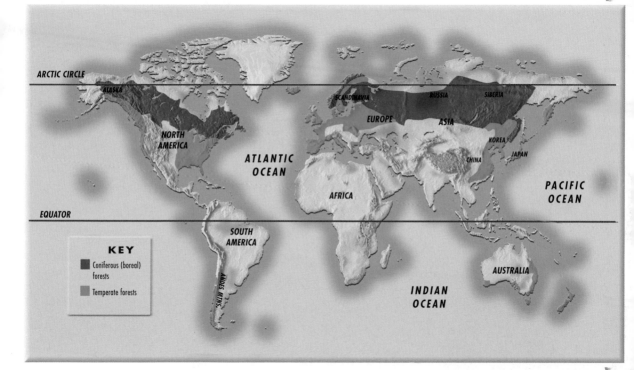

ARCTIC CIRCLE

ALASKA

SCANDINAVIA
RUSSIA
SIBERIA

EUROPE
ASIA

NORTH
AMERICA

KOREA
JAPAN

ATLANTIC
OCEAN

CHINA

PACIFIC
OCEAN

AFRICA

EQUATOR

SOUTH
AMERICA

INDIAN
OCEAN

AUSTRALIA

ANDES MTNS.

KEY

■ Coniferous (boreal) forests

■ Temperate forests

MONKEY PUZZLE FORESTS

The ancestors of today's monkey puzzle trees grew millions of years ago in the days of the dinosaurs. Monkey puzzle trees are now found in the wild only in the Andes Mountains of southeastern Chile (*right*). Monkey puzzles rise as high as 150 feet (45 m). Their rigid, overlapping needlelike leaves grow in spirals around stiff branches. The resulting prickly, tangled network discourages animals from climbing the tree. Chilean forests are home to the Pehuenche people, who consider the trees sacred. Their name comes from *pehuan*, their name for the monkey puzzle tree. They do not cut the trees down but gather the seeds to grind into flour.

CONIFEROUS FORESTS

The great boreal forests are sometimes called the taiga, a Russian word most likely derived from a Siberian language. The evergreen, needle-bearing trees of the taiga belong to the conifers – an ancient group that produce their seeds in cones. They appeared on Earth some 300 million years ago, long before flowering plants. Coniferous trees are superb, year-round wind deflectors, so the interior of the forest is often sheltered from even the fiercest winter blizzards. But little light penetrates through to the forest floor, and the dry layer of needles on the ground does not encourage seed germination. Fungi do well because they do not need light to grow. But only a few small plants, such as ferns and mosses, can survive in the gloom beneath the trees. Wildflowers and berry bushes, such as bilberry and juniper, thrive in clearings and natural gaps in the trees. Lakes are common, occurring in hollows in the ground that were gouged out by glaciers during the last ice age. The ground is often waterlogged because of the low evaporation of water and slow rates of decomposition in the cold climate.

WHY NEEDLES?

Most conifers have long, thin, needle-shaped leaves, making it difficult for snow to accumulate and weigh down the branches (*above*). They contain very little sap, so there is little liquid to freeze. They tend to be dark in color in order to absorb the maximum amount of heat from feeble sunshine. They don't lose much water because they have a waxy surface and only a few breathing pores, hidden in the bottom of grooves along the length of the needles. Reducing water loss is important because roots cannot absorb water when the soil is frozen.

WINTER SURVIVAL

During winter some animals from the cold Arctic and tundra lands migrate south to shelter in conifererous forests. Packs of wolves (*left, right*) may follow their prey, caribou (reindeer), into the forests. Forest residents such as woodchucks and bats hibernate through the winter, while bears doze to save energy. Many birds migrate south to warmer climates and return in spring.

FEEDING ON CONES

The tough, waxy needles of conifers are difficult to eat, and most animals leave them alone. The seeds in the cones, however, are a vital source of nourishment. The crossbill (*left*) has an extraordinary crossed beak to help it pry the protein-rich seeds from cones. It may collect as many as a thousand seeds a day. A bigger bird called a nutcracker can crush cones with a straightforward bite to release the seeds.

TREE SHAPES

Firs and spruces, such as Colorado spruces (*right*), are shaped like cathedral spires, while pines tend to be less compact. These trees' shapes, and flexible branches, encourage snow to slide easily from down-swept branches. If the snow were to build up, the branches might break under its weight.

FIRE FORESTS

Fire is common in coniferous forests (*left*). The thick carpet of needles on the forest floor often ignites when lightning strikes in the course of a long, dry summer. Conifer trees tend to have thick, fibrous bark that helps them resist fires. The cones of some conifers, such as giant redwoods, release their seeds only during the heat of a forest fire. Some pine trees in California need the fierce heat to make their seeds germinate, or sprout. Because conifers grow close together, fires spread quickly among them and are hard to fight. Water is sometimes dropped on the trees from helicopters.

MAMMAL PREDATORS

Mammals are relatively scarce in northern forests, so predators, such as bobcats (*above*), sometimes have to cover vast distances to get food. Bobcats feed at night mainly on small rodents, such as lemmings and voles, and on birds and carrion. Their thick fur helps them keep warm.

Imagine walking through a forest so tall that the treetops seem lost in the sky. Their furrowed, russet-red trunks are planted firmly in the ground, and some are so wide you could drive a car through a tunnel cut into them. These are the redwood trees of California, also called sequoias, thought to be named after the American Indian leader Sequoyah, who invented the Cherokee alphabet. Extremely old, they are still standing tall after 3,000 years – 40 human lifetimes. Their vast size is partly due to the fertile soil and humid conditions of the U.S. west coast, where the trees grow in river valleys. A broad network of roots provides an enormous surface area for taking in enough moisture and nutrients for a tree to maintain a huge crown. One giant sequoia yields about 1,500-2,000 new cones a year and can still produce cones when it is thousands of years old.

THICK SKIN

Redwood trees have reddish wood at the heart of the trunk and cinnamon-red colored bark (*left*), which is thick. Giant sequoia bark may exceed 24 inches (60 cm) in places, making it the thickest bark on Earth. The thickness of redwoods' bark helps the trees reach great ages. The bark is soft and fibrous and also a poor conductor of heat, so the trees have some built-in fire protection.

TREE HOUSES

Carpenter ants (*left*) live in colonies in the bark and dead wood of living trees such as sequoias and in stumps, logs, and dead trees. They chew tunnels through the bark with their strong mandibles (mouthparts) to make brood chambers for their young. The ground underneath a nest is usually a mass of reddish sawdust. Colony chambers may be as long as 20 feet (6 m). The tunnels do not really damage the tree, but they may allow other insects and agents of decay to enter. They also let air into the bark, which dries it out and makes it more likely to catch fire.

EATING AND SLEEPING

American black bears (*left*) are common in redwood and other North American forests. They are active at night, and roam long distances in search of fruit, berries, nuts, roots, and honey. In autumn they gorge themselves on fruit to store enough body fat to last them through the winter. Bears do not really hibernate but sleep in dens for 20-30 weeks of the year. Cubs are born in January or February and stay in the den with their mother until spring.

RED FLYER

Roosting in redwood trees during the day, red bats (*right*) emerge at night to feed on insects. This species is unusual among bats in having three or four young. Most bats have only one or two young. At first, the female carries her young with her, even though their combined body weight may exceed her own weight. Red bats are warm-weather visitors and migrate southward in winter.

SECRETIVE SNAKE

The western diamondback (*right*), the most adaptable of U.S. rattlesnakes, is found on prairies and by streams as well as in redwood forests.

It has a dramatic threat display (behavior aimed at deterring opponents): it raises its head and neck high above the ground in a tight S-curve and prominently exhibits its black-and-white tail. The buzzing sound of the tail rattle is designed to frighten enemies.

WHY LEAVES FALL

Deciduous trees lose their leaves to help them survive the winter.

WINTER

In winter there is not much sunlight, and water in the ground may be frozen. Without these two vital ingredients, trees cannot photosynthesize (make food), so they shut down and become dormant.

SPRING/SUMMER

With spring rains and warmer, sunnier days, the trees come back to life. They grow new leaves and flowers.

AUTUMN

In autumn the trees take nutrients from the leaves back into the branches and trunks. The leaves change color as they dry up, and they eventually fall off the tree.

VOLE ATTACK

Many rodents live in deciduous woods, including the bank voles of Europe (*right*) and the jumping mice of North America. Bank voles are good climbers and often bite off tree bark to feed on the tree's living layer just beneath it. Bank voles may damage trees when food is scarce, but field voles are a real danger. They sometimes chew a ring of bark right around the tree, which cuts off its food and water supply and it dies.

LADY KILLERS

The wide, juicy leaves found on most deciduous trees make better meals than conifer needles, and many insects and other animals eat them. But predators lurk among the leaves. Ladybugs (*left*) and their larvae eat small insects such as aphids. The beetles' name arose in the Middle Ages, when they were thought to be associated with "Our Lady" (the Virgin Mary) because they helped rid crops of insect pests.

WOODY WOODPECKER

The rapid drumming noise of a woodpecker's bill against a tree trunk (*right*) as it digs out food or a nest is a characteristic sound in deciduous woods. With the sound the bird also proclaims its territory and attracts a mate. Woodpeckers have long, curved claws to cling to tree trunks and a short stiff tail that acts as a prop. Their bills are sharply pointed so they can chisel into tree trunks and find insects, which they lick up with a long, sticky tongue. In some species, the tongue is as long as the bird's own body.

DECIDUOUS FORESTS

Warm summers, cool winters, and fairly even rainfall throughout the year provide ideal conditions for deciduous trees such as oaks, beeches, chestnuts, maples, and ashes. Species in North American forests are more varied than in Europe and include aspen, linden, hickory, magnolia, and buckeye as well as oak, beech, and maple. There is plenty of water and sunshine available in the summer months. The trees' broad leaves spread, layer upon layer, to catch as much sunshine as possible. Deciduous forests are lighter and more open than coniferous forests, and more plants grow on the forest floor. Yet deciduous forests are still dominated by the seasons. Spring and summer are times of plant growth and the birth of young animals. In the autumn some trees lose their leaves, and animals eat well and store food for the winter. Winter is a time of hibernation, migration, or a struggle to find food.

TREE LEAVES

The leaves of most deciduous trees are wide and flat (*above*) – which helps them catch the Sun's light energy. They combine this with carbon dioxide from the air and water from the soil to make sugars, which are food for the tree. This process is called photosynthesis.

NEW ARRIVALS

Young animals, such as white-tailed deer fawns, are often born in spring, when there is plenty to eat. They then have the summer to grow fit and strong before winter. The fawn's spotted coat (*right*) helps camouflage it among the trees; although all deer are difficult to see in forests because of their brown colors and the way they move so quietly among the trees.

FOREST PLANTS

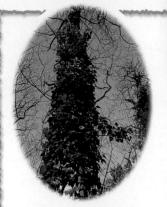

Deciduous forests grow in three basic layers. The tallest trees – such as oak, beech, maple, and lime – provide the upper canopy of leaves. Holly, willows, hazel, and other shorter trees and shrubs grow in the middle. At the bottom is the field, or herbaceous, layer of flowering plants, ferns, and mosses. To survive in the shade of the bigger trees, some plants climb up them or perch on their branches to get nearer to the light. After the upper canopy of leaves has fallen, more light reaches the evergreen plants, such as holly, and they continue to grow in winter. On the forest floor are plants with large leaves – size is helpful in trapping light – or plants that feed on other creatures, both living and dead, and so do not need light to make their own food. Coniferous forests tend to have two, rather than three, layers of plant life because the trees cast such deep shade. The damp soils of forests are ideal habitats for ferns and mosses, which need moisture to reproduce. Fallen leaves and dead wood build up on the forest floor and provide rich nutrients for plants to recycle. Fungi are particularly important in the recycling process.

GREEN CLIMBER

Common, or English, ivy (*above*) climbs up trees using special adhesive roots. The roots are so fine they can find a grip in the tiniest crevice in bark. The ivy sticks to the tree, but there is no evidence that the tree supplies it with any nourishment. Since ivy leaves are evergreen, they can carry out photosynthesis even in winter. Ivy is one of the few plants that flower in the fall. It is pollinated by insects, such as flies and wasps, and grows blackish berrylike fruits over the winter. Birds may eat the berries in spring and help scatter the seeds.

LAYERS OF A FOREST

A deciduous forest can be divided into three main layers.

CANOPY
The highest level, made up of mature trees

SHRUB LAYER, OR UNDERSTORY
Made up of bushes, shrubs, and young trees

FIELD LAYER
A carpet of flowers, herbs, ferns, and mosses on the forest foor

The forest floor is covered with leaf litter – decaying leaves and plant debris – and fungi.

FOREST FUNGI

Unlike green plants, fungi (*right*) cannot make their own food. They absorb nutrients from plant sugars or from other organisms, including organisms that have died. The large amount of dead and decaying material in woodlands is an ideal food source for fungi. Many of them live in partnership with trees, taking some sugars from them but also helping the trees to absorb minerals from the soil.

SPRINGING TO LIFE

Fire in this coniferous forest (*right*) has allowed more light to reach the forest floor, and a yellow carpet of heartleaf arnica has spread luxuriantly. A single species of plant may grow over a large area if it reproduces vegetatively from underground stems. Many flowering plants, such as bluebells and wood sorrel, sprout rapidly in spring before the trees come into full leaf and shade the forest floor. They store food in underground structures such as bulbs, corms, tubers, or rhizomes, and so are ready to grow quickly in spring.

NESTING ORCHID

The bird's-nest orchid (*left*), found in Eurasia, is named for its thick, tangled mass of roots. It grows in the thick layers of leaf litter in deciduous forests, especially under beech trees. Lacking the green pigment (chlorophyll) required for photosynthesis, it obtains its nourishment from dead and decaying plant matter.

FERN LIFE CYCLE

A fern produces spores in sacs called sori, located on the underside (*right*) of the fern's fronds, or leaves. The spores do not grow into new fern plants but into a tiny, heart-shaped structure called a prothallus, which produces sperm and egg cells. A sperm cell has to swim through moisture to fuse with an egg cell before a new fern plant can develop. In winter, fern plants die back, and the dead fronds protect the growing tip of the plant during the most severe weather.

BIG MOUTH

Tawny frogmouths (a type of large nightjar) are well camouflaged by day. When they keep very still and upright, their streaked and speckled feathers look like broken branches (*above*). At night, the frogmouth glides down from its perch to catch beetles, centipedes, frogs, and mice in its beak. A tuft of stiff feathers at the base of the bill acts like a cat's whiskers to help the bird find its way or to sense food in the dark.

EUCALYPTUS FORESTS

From noisy, brightly colored birds by day, to secretive furry mammals at night, Australian eucalyptus forests are home to a variety of fascinating and unique wildlife. The air is filled with the buzzing and chirping of insects and the sweet, powerful scents of eucalyptus leaves and acacia flowers. Dry bark hangs from the eucalyptus trunks in long curling strips. Eventually it falls to the ground and mixes with fallen leaves, making a crunchy carpet underfoot. The climate in these unusual forests is seasonal, with rain falling mainly in the winter months. Rainwater collects in marshy pools, creating a habitat for frogs, snakes, and water birds, such as ibises, pelicans, black swans, and ducks. Many birds, such as honeyeaters and lorikeets, and mammals, such as honey possums and bats, feed on the nectar and pollen in the eucalyptus trees and in shrubs such as grevilleas and banksias. Parrots use their strong bills to crack open seeds. Insects are also a plentiful source of food for other wildlife.

FURRY PARACHUTE

Webs of furry skin between the front and back legs of a sugar glider (*left*) spread out like a parachute when it jumps from tree to tree. Sugar gliders can cover distances as great as 180 feet (55 m) in one glide and land with a quiet plopping sound. They feed on insects, nectar, fruit, and the sweet, sugary sap of wattle (acacia) and gum (eucalyptus) trees. Using their sharp front teeth they gnaw at the bark to reach the sap beneath it.

NO DRINK

The koala (*left*) gets its name from an Australian aboriginal word meaning "no drink"– the animal obtains most of its moisture from its food and rarely drinks. Koalas eat only the leaves of certain types of eucalyptus trees. The animal has cheek pouches in which to store the leaves and an extra long intestine to help digest them. Koalas have claws like knives that help them cling to branches, as well as long fingers and toes to help them climb.

LEAF EATER

The brightly patterned caterpillar of the emperor gum moth (*above*) is surprisingly well camouflaged among the young leaves of the eucalyptus trees on which it feeds. The caterpillar makes a cocoon, from which it emerges as a handsome moth with eyespots on its back wings. These startle and confuse predators, such as birds, and draw attention away from the moth's vulnerable head.

STICKY TOES

With its long, thin sticky toes, White's tree frog (*right*) can grip wet leaves and other slippery surfaces, such as tree trunks after rain. Its belly skin is very loose, giving it a better grip when climbing. The green skin color blends in well with the forest, where the frog hides during the day. At night, it hunts for beetles, moths, and other small cratures, catching them in its wide mouth.

OAK LEAF SAP

OAK LEAF APHID

GREAT TIT

SPARROW HAWK

*The juicy leaves
of deciduous trees
provide tasty snacks
for an army of insects
in the summer
months. Small birds
rely on these insects to
feed both themselves
and their ever-hungry
young. They are, in
turn, preyed upon by
larger birds, such as
sparrow hawks.*

PREDATORS AND PREY

Forest predators come in all shapes and sizes –
from tiny spiders and beetles in leaf litter to
huge owls and tigers. Swooping through the trees
are birds such as owls, sparrow hawks, goshawks, and, in
Australia, crested hawks. Among the branches are martens,
Australian western quolls, and insect-eating birds such
as woodpeckers, pied flycatchers, and solitary vireos. The
northern shrike of coniferous woods has a strongly hooked
bill for catching frogs and grasshoppers in summer and
finches and mice in winter. Larger hunters – such as the
Siberian tiger, lynx, bobcat, red fox, and wolverine – stalk
their prey on the forest floor, often patrolling large areas
to find enough food. Lynx on the hunt may range over
125 square miles (200 sq km). Prowling in the leaf litter
are smaller hunters, such as salamanders, toads, snakes,
shrews, wolf spiders, daddy longlegs, ground
beetles, and predatory fly larvae.

CRAFTY COYOTE

Coyotes (*left*) eat a lot of small mammals,
including squirrels, rabbits, and mice. Individual
coyotes hunt small prey by themselves, but they
work together to bring down larger animals such
as deer and bighorns (Rocky Mountain sheep).
Two or more coyotes may chase larger prey
for up to 1,300 feet (400 m).

EIGHT-LEGGED WOLF

Although they are not social animals and do not hunt in packs like wolves, many wolf spiders (*left*) do chase their prey. They detect its movement with their eyes and with sensitive hairs that pick up vibrations. A high-speed dash often ends with the spider hurling itself onto its victim. Its powerful digestive juices can liquefy small prey within minutes. Wolf spiders can be regarded as cannibals because they sometimes eat members of their own species.

SUPER SWOOPERS

Woodland owls (*left*) have short, rounded wings. While hunting, they sit quietly on a low perch, watching and listening for small mammals. Hearing a likely noise, they silently swoop down, swinging their feet forward at the last moment to hit the prey, often killing it outright.

AERIAL ACROBAT

Martens (*right*) leap and bound effortlessly from branch to branch in pursuit of prey such as birds and squirrels. Their bushy tails help them keep their balance, and their large, hairy paws and sharp claws grip the branches well. Martens inspect the likely hiding places of their prey. If they find a potential meal, they kill it with a bite to the back of the neck.

BIGGEST TIGER

The Siberian tiger (*right*), the world's biggest cat, hunts in the coniferous forests of northern Asia. Its enormous body and long, shaggy fur help it conserve heat and keep warm in the snow. Like all tigers, Siberian tigers hunt alone. They stalk their prey to within 65 feet (20 m) and then knock it over with the weight of their body or a swipe of their huge paws. A bite to the throat usually suffocates the prey. A Siberian tiger can eat over 75 pounds (35 kilograms) of meat in just one meal.

CONIFER FOREST FOOD CHAIN

FIR TREE

FUNGI

RED SQUIRREL

MARTEN

The fungi in coniferous woods feed on dead and decaying trees. They are, in turn, eaten by red squirrels or other fungivores (fungus eaters). Carnivores (meat eaters), such as martens, prey on squirrels and other small animals.

DEFENSE

In the "eat-and-be-eaten" world of forests, animals have developed cunning methods of survival. Some, such as grass snakes and opossums, pretend to be dead, since most predators, preferring to eat living prey, will leave them alone. Others are protected by sharp spines, poisons, or armor. If the animal has armor only on its back, it may roll into a tight ball to protect its soft belly. Hedgehogs, echidnas, and pill bugs (a type of wood louse) do this to deter predators. When striped skunks are threatened, they do a handstand and spray a smelly liquid on their attacker. Lobster moth caterpillars may squirt formic acid at their attackers. Puss moth caterpillars make use of a more passive method of defense: huge fake eye markings that make them look dangerous. Other passive methods include camouflage, hiding, and running away.

CAMOUFLAGE

This *Arsenura* moth (*left and above*) could easily be mistaken for just another fallen leaf. It even has lines along its wings that look like the veins on leaves and help break up the outline of its body. In coniferous forests, many caterpillars avoid detection by closely matching the color and shape of pine needles.

TIGHTROPE TRICKS

At the slightest sign of danger, squirrels take to the trees, leaping gracefully from branch to branch and using their long tail as a rudder. Running up and down smooth tree trunks and balancing on the flimsiest twigs is easy for them. On the ground, squirrels often stop, sit upright, and sniff the air. If they detect any possible danger, they use their tail to signal a warning to other squirrels.

DEAD OR ALIVE

When a North American opossum (*right*) is under threat, it will often open its mouth and curl back its lips to reveal its 50 sharp teeth. Another defense strategy it uses is to "play dead" by rolling over onto its back with its tongue hanging out. The opossum may stay in this trancelike state for hours.

SPINY COAT

The Australian echidna (*left*), or spiny anteater, relies on its sharp, spiny coat for protection. If alarmed, it may roll into a spiky ball. When disturbed in the open, it burrows straight down, using sharp claws and great heaves of its powerful body. Echidnas are brainy, too. They perform very well in laboratory tests designed to test learning, memory, and other advanced mental processes. In some tests they do better than cats, so they may be able to use their wits to avoid danger.

BEWARE, POISON!

The brightly colored spots and stripes of Europe's fire salamander (*right*) warn predators to leave it alone. The animal's skin secretes a poison that will irritate a predator's mouth and eyes and is powerful enough to kill small mammals. The poison glands are located at the top of the head.

GLUED TO THE SPOT

Even trees have their own defense. If a conifer tree is damaged, sticky resin oozes out of the wound to seal the cut and protect the tree from attack by fungi and insects. This deerfly (*left*) has been caught in the resin from a white pine tree. Insects from millions of years ago have been found perfectly preserved in amber (hardened resin).

NIGHTTIME ANIMALS

The rich resources of forest and woodland habitats are used 24 hours a day. As the Sun sets and most birds settle down to roost, an immense variety of night creatures emerge from their daytime hiding places. Animals come out at night to take advantage of the cool, moist night air and to avoid predators – although some predators hunt only at night. These nighttime predators have keen senses of sight, hearing, and smell to help them find their way around and locate food. Some, such as badgers, have a special layer at the back of the eye that reflects as much light as possible into the eye. The long, sensitive whiskers of mice and other rodents are useful for feeling their way through undergrowth in the dark. Nighttime, or nocturnal, animals are often well camouflaged in order to hide themselves from danger during the day.

SILENT HUNTER

The tawny owl (*left*) is hard to see during the day because its mottled brown feathers blend in well with tree bark and leaves. At night its keen hearing and silent flight make it an excellent hunter. Fluffy, comblike fringes on its feathers deaden the sound of its wing beats. The velvety surface of its feathers muffles the sound made by their brushing against one another and by the air rushing between them.

NIGHTTIME RAMBLERS

Wood lice (*right*) are usually out and about at night when forests are damp and cool. They often climb trees in search of lichens and algae to eat. Unlike insects, wood lice lack a waterproof cuticle (body case), so they cannot afford to lose too much water. They instinctively move away from the light and come to rest in damp, dark places.

HIDDEN MOTHS

To avoid being spotted by the many birds hunting in the woods by day, most forest moths are well camouflaged. Their front wings resemble their daytime resting places. The merveille du jour moth (*left*) is almost invisible when sitting on lichen-covered bark. Lappet and angleshades moths look like dead leaves. Green moths, such as the green silver line or the emerald, can easily hide among fresh green leaves.

BEETLE HUNTER

The greater horseshoe bat (*left*) is slow and fluttering in flight and not good at catching insects in the air. It flies and feeds quite low to the ground, swooping down on beetles, such as cockchafers in spring and dor beetles later in the year. It navigates in the dark by producing high-pitched squeaks through its nose while keeping its mouth shut. Echoes bounce back and inform the bat of the position of nearby objects and whether or not they are moving.

MASTER DIGGERS

Eurasian badgers (*left*) spend most of the day underground, out of sight in their sett, a network of tunnels and chambers they dig with their strong legs and claws. At dusk a badger emerges from its sett for a night of hunting. Badgers are especially fond of earthworms but eat a variety of insects, rabbits, carrion (creatures already dead), and fruit. Shallow holes near a sett are where a badger has dug for food, and well-worn paths trace the extent of its territory.

FANTASTIC FAN

The male superb lyrebird (*above*) of Australia has two broad, lyre-shaped tail feathers and a mass of long, silvery plumes. Having raked up a mound of soil, he dances and sings on it to attract females for mating and to drive away rival males. During this courtship display, his long tail feathers spread out and arch forward in a shimmering fan shape to impress a passing female.

COURTSHIP

In spring and autumn, forests echo with the sounds of animal courtship. Sound is a useful means of communication as it can be easily heard even when animals are hidden among leaves and branches. Many birds migrate to the forests of the northern hemisphere in spring for courtship and nesting. The beautiful birdsong that fills these woodlands in spring is designed to attract a mate or claim a territory. Feather displays are used to impress the mate, when in view. Woodpeckers even use trees as natural drums to send messages to potential mates or rivals. In the autumn, male deer roar out a throaty challenge to their rivals and clash their antlers in spectacular fights over herds of females. They grow new antlers every year. Insects are not usually as noisy as birds or mammals, relying more on scents and colors during courtship.

FEATHERED DRUMMER

In spring the male ruffed grouse (*left*) often sits on a log and makes a drumming sound by beating his wings to and fro. The sound carries a long way through a coniferous forest and helps attract a female for mating. During his loud display the male also spreads out his tail like a fan.

CRICKET CALLS

In the darkness of a forest night, the male oak bush cricket repeatedly drums one of his back legs against a leaf to attract a female. He raises his wings to make the drumming sounds louder. Females (*left*) pick up the drumming sounds of the males through ears on their front legs and move toward the male of their choice. Both sexes have ears, but only the males can drum.

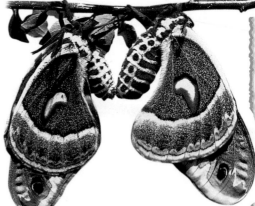

MATING MOTHS

Male cecropia moths (*above*) have lots of branches along their feathery antennae. Tiny hairs along these branches catch the scent of female cecropia moths from long distances away. The female gives off a mating scent at night, and the male follows the scent trail to find the female.

PANDA PARTNERS

Male and female giant pandas each live alone in the bamboo forests of southwest China (*left*). In spring the pandas may look for a mate. When a female panda is ready to mate, she lets the male panda know by leaving scent marks on logs and stones, and she makes bleating and grunting noises. A male panda answers her calls and may roar to warn other males to keep away. A pair of mating pandas stay together for just a few days, then each goes its own way.

WOOD DRILL

Ichneumon wasps (*above*) lay their eggs in or near the larvae of other bugs. For example, some types drill holes into pine trees to lay their eggs on larvae of the wood wasp. The female's egg-laying tube, or ovipositor, is longer than her body and thus can reach wood wasp larvae hidden deep within pine trees. She is able to drill a hole 1¼ inches (3 cm) deep in solid wood in less than 20 minutes. After hatching, the ichneumon larvae feed on the wood wasp larvae.

NESTS, EGGS, AND YOUNG

In a forest there are plenty of places to hide the young and keep them warm. Even so, there may be fierce competition for the best nesting sites. Birds sing loudly to claim the territory in which they feed and breed. Tree holes make protective nest sites for birds such as owls and woodpeckers, while other birds and squirrels prefer to build nests high in the branches. Hollow trees make ideal roosting and hibernation sites for woodland bats. Other mammals nest among tree roots or in burrows concealed by leaf litter. Some small mammals, such as lemmings, breed very quickly. One female lemming may have thirty to forty young in a season, and some of those young may breed when they are only 19 days old. The forest floor is alive with them in years when the weather is good and food is plentiful. The trees also swarm with caterpillars and other insect young in spring and summer, providing a supply of food for hungry bird nestlings. Some insects lay their eggs in leaves or nuts or deep inside tree trunks. Wood is not very nutritious, so those that eat it take a long time to grow.

CAMOUFLAGE COAT

Female wild boars give birth to a litter of up to ten striped young (*left*) in spring or early summer. The stripes help camouflage the young, enabling them to blend into the dappled light and shade of the woods. One or two adult sows live together with their young of various ages. Adult males live alone or in small bachelor groups that stay close to the females and their young.

BABY CARRIER

Female red-necked pademelons (*right*) are smaller than the males. This marsupial, found in Australia, has four teats in a pouch that opens forward on her body. She rears a single young, or joey, which stays in the pouch for about 26 weeks of suckling. It is tiny and undeveloped when born, but it is kept warm, safe, and fed inside the pouch.

VOLE CONTROL

Great gray owls (*right*) feed almost entirely on small mammals, especially voles. These small rodents tend to increase in number over a period of a few years, and then the number falls catastrophically. When there are lots of voles, the well-fed owls produce bigger and bigger broods, or clutches. Eventually, they may lay seven, eight, or even nine eggs in a clutch. In years when there are few voles, great gray owls may lay only one or two eggs. If the owls face starvation, they leave the northern forests and travel south in search of food.

CUTE CUBS

Brown bears, such as grizzly bears, mate in May or June, and the cubs are born ten months later during winter. The mother gives birth in a cave, hollow tree, or other sheltered spot. She and the cubs do not venture out of the den until April or June. The cubs weigh only about 12-14 ounces (350-400 grams) when born. They have hardly any fur and are quite helpless, but they grow fast on their mother's rich milk. Mother and cubs (*below*) stay together for 1½–4½ years. The age at which the female gives birth, the litter size, and the interval between litters are controlled by the amount and quality of her diet.

LIVING TOGETHER

WOOD ANTS

Colonies of wood ants may contain several thousand to half a million ants or more. They range widely over trees in search of insects, such as beetles (*above*), to take back to their nest. A big colony may eat up to 100,000 insects and larvae in a day. The nest is made of a pile of pine needles, small sticks, and other debris and may be as large as 5 feet (1.5 m) high and 10 feet (3 m) across. Underground is a deep network of corridors and chambers. In most nests there are several large queen ants laying eggs, with workers cleaning and feeding the larvae. Guard ants squirt enemies with formic acid. On warm spring and summer days, clouds of winged males and females emerge from the nest. After mating, the fertilized queens fly off to found a new colony, or in some cases may rejoin their home nest.

Living together in organized social groups is mutually beneficial to many woodland animals, such as deer, wild boars, bats, and wood ants. The individuals in a group help each other spot danger, find food, and rear the young. In mammal societies experienced adults may pass on survival skills to younger, immature members of the group. Insect societies are highly organized, with individual castes carrying out different tasks, such as gathering food or guarding the nest. Some birds, such as American red-cockaded woodpeckers, live in groups where only one pair actually nests. The others, usually younger relatives, take turns guarding the nest hole. They may also help feed the young. Associations between different types of living things are common in forests. Ambrosia beetles chew into wood to make tunnels, where they farm fungi, which they eat. The fungi feed on beetle droppings, changing any undigested wood into a form the beetles can eat.

LAZY CUCKOOS

In many types of Eurasian cuckoos, the female lays her eggs in other birds' nests; her eggs often have colors and markings matching the host bird's eggs. When the cuckoo chick hatches after 12 days, it quickly gets rid of the other eggs and chicks so it can have all the food its foster parents bring. The baby cuckoo (*above*) manipulates each egg and chick into its hollowed-out back and tips its load over the rim of the nest!

A SIMPLE ANTS' NEST

Larvae spin cocoons, in which they pass the pre-adult pupal life stage.

Workers move pupae around to keep them at an even temperature.

An entrance to the nest can be closed in cold or rainy weather, or to control nest temperature.

Eggs hatch into larvae. Workers clean and feed them.

Rubbish chamber

Queen lays eggs.

Queen's chamber. She is larger than the workers.

Food chamber

RED DEER

Red deer (*above*), known as wapiti or elk in North America, are sociable animals, but the adult males and females live apart except during the October mating season. One herd is made up of a mature female, her female relatives, and their dependent young of both sexes. Herds of adult males have a hierarchy of importance. The buck who is strongest and has the biggest and best antlers is the dominant male, but he loses his place in the hierarchy when he sheds his antlers sometime between March and June. When all the males have shed their antlers, there is no hierarchy. It is reestablished when their antlers grow again.

GALL MAKERS

Strange growths called galls (*left*) develop on many woodland plants. Most are caused by gall wasps, but others by beetles, flies, and mites that lay their eggs inside leaves, buds, or twigs. When the larvae hatch, their presence stimulates the surrounding plant tissue to grow into a variety of weirdly shaped galls. Each gall contains one or more developing larvae. In some, the adult insect emerges in the summer. In others, the gall turns brown and the larvae inside hibernate through the winter. There will often be other insects within the gall, some of them parasites. The oak apple gall has been known to house 75 different species of insect as well as the gall wasp grub.

PEOPLE AND FORESTS

For thousands of years forests were feared because predatory animals lived in them, but forests were also relied on as a rich source of food and natural materials. Many traditional peoples were entirely dependent on forests. They respected the trees and other living creatures and took only what they needed. They were themselves part of a finely balanced ecosystem. Most of these peoples now live in industrial societies, and many of their forests have been destroyed; only traces of their ways and knowledge remain. Nowadays, forests provide products rather than shelter for people. Timber is harvested, often grown in special plantations. Cork is harvested from the bark of cork oaks in Portugal and elsewhere – it can be stripped off about every ten years without harming the trees. Fruit and fungi are also harvested in many countries. But forests also provide many people with a chance to enjoy activities such as cycling, hiking, bird-watching, and orienteering.

FROM FORESTS TO FARMS

Many forests in Europe and North America have been reduced to small clumps of trees in the middle of cultivated fields (*above*). Trees are slow to grow and hard to harvest. Few landowners can afford to wait 50 years or more to make money from a tree crop. Forests tend to survive on steeply sloping land that is unsuitable for plowing or where people still use trees for firewood or other traditional purposes.

WOODEN HOUSES

Nowadays, forests are used mainly to provide timber for buildings and furniture. This log cabin in an aspen forest (*left*) is constructed entirely of wood, but even brick or stone houses usually have wooden frameworks and roof supports. A lot of building timber and wood for making paper is grown in renewable plantations. Fast-growing tree species in such plantations are typically planted in straight lines to make them easier and faster to harvest. Plantations are not as rich in wildlife as natural woodlands.

TRUFFLE HUNTING

Pigs and dogs are trained to sniff out truffles (*right*), an edible fungus that grows, in partnership with tree roots, at depths of about 12 inches (30 cm). To disperse their spores, truffles attract animals by producing some of the scents made by the animals. The fungi range in size from as small as a pea to as big as an orange, and many are considered a delicacy, especially the black Périgord truffle and the white Piedmont truffle from France and Italy.

TRANSPORTING WOOD

Trees are bulky and difficult to move, and so they have traditionally been transported via rivers. The areas most heavily logged were those with large rivers, and forests remote from rivers used to survive untouched. Pulp mills (*left*) are often located at the mouth of a river, especially where it enters a lake that can be used to store floating logs. Large trucks are now often used to transport logs, so forests far from rivers are being exploited.

TOTEM POLES

This Kwakiutl chief (*right*) from Canada's Pacific coast region is wearing an eagle headdress. The Kwakiutl people traditionally built villages of wooden houses and were famous for their arts, particularly their totem poles. Carved from trees within the tribal boundaries, the poles depict animals that have a special relationship with the spirits and way of life of the community. If an animal is symbolized on a totem, then typically it will be one which the tribe will not eat or has special reverence for. Through such symbols and spirit beliefs many tribes express their deep relationship with the natural environment.

PROTECTING FORESTS

The forests of Earth's temperate zones are vital to life on the planet. They affect the balance of water and gases in the atmosphere, prevent soil erosion, and are home to a wide variety of wildlife. But only a fraction of the original temperate forests remain. The United Nations Food and Agriculture Organization reported in 2005 that the problem of forest loss in the temperate zones appeared to be easing, with some countries even reporting an increase in forest area. Serious concerns, however, remain. Pollution, such as acid rain, takes a toll, particularly in coniferous forests. Fires and fungus diseases also cause a lot of damage. More could be done to save the remaining temperate-zone forests and use them sustainably: cork can be harvested; trees can be coppiced (cut so they grow again); new trees can be planted to replace those cut down; and pollution can be reduced to lessen the amount of acid rain.

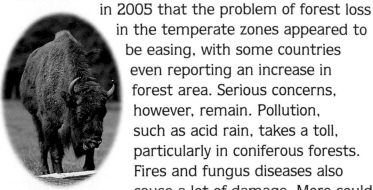

BISON REFUGE

The great Bialowieza forest in Poland and Belarus is one of the last wild woodlands left in Europe. The European bison, or wisent, became extinct in the wild in the early 20th century but was later reintroduced into the Bialowieza forest from zoo collections. This bison (*above*) at a breeding center in Poland will eventually be released into the forest.

FOREST FIRES

Forest fires (*left*) can be beneficial or harmful. Natural fires in small areas are essential to trigger seed germination for some tree species, and to create open spaces where new trees can grow. But large-scale fires, often carelessly started by cigarettes or campfires, are hard to control and cause terrible destruction to trees and their associated wildlife. People who use forests need to be aware of the fire risk.

SAVE THE PANDA

As of 2004, the number of giant pandas left in the wild was estimated to be only about 1,600. They are difficult to breed in captivity. This female (*left*) is being artificially inseminated at a Chinese breeding center; she may have one or two cubs. Pandas were more common centuries ago when there were bamboo forests all over China. But the forests were cut down to build villages and provide land for rice crops, and pandas were hunted for their skins. They are now protected in reserves, and it is illegal to kill them. However, they remain an endangered species.

COPPICING

Coppicing is a way to harvest timber without felling all the trees. This method, which works with certain species, involves cutting the trees down to a stump (*right*). Several new shoots grow from the stump instead of one trunk, and they can be harvested after several years. Hazel and sweet chestnut are examples of trees that may be harvested in this fashion. Coppiced woods are light and open, thereby encouraging the growth of flowering plants on the forest floor.

FUTURE WOODS

This hiker (*left*) walking along a nature trail in a U.S. forest will gain a greater understanding of the importance of forests to wildlife. Our forests will survive in the future only if we understand more about the way they work, appreciate how and why they are threatened, and do more to preserve existing forests and create new ones.

ACID RAIN

Vast areas of forest in Europe and North America are seriously threatened by acid rain. Acid rain is precipitation that is more acidic than normal as a result of the release into the air of smoke and chemical fumes from motor vehicles, power stations, and industry (*right*). Acid rain caused in one country may be blown by the wind to another. Trees in southern Canada are harmed by acid rain created in the northern United States. Pollution from Western Europe poses a threat to trees in southern Norway and Sweden. Acid rain can be lethal for coniferous forests, since their soils tend to be naturally acidic and thus can do little to neutralize the acidity of the rain; the acid rain consequently leads to the release of toxic aluminium into the soil, thereby poisoning tree roots.

FOR FURTHER INFORMATION

*The followng are some of the sources available that can help you find out more
about forests in the temperate zones of the world and the plants, wildlife, and people living in them.*

Books

Allaby, Michael, and Richard Garratt. *Temperate Forests*. Biomes of the Earth series (Facts on File)

Butterfield, Moira. *Protecting Temperate Forests* (Gareth Stevens)

Henry, J. David. *Canada's Boreal Forest* (Smithsonian)

Kricher, John, and C. Gordon Morrison. *Peterson First Guide to Forests* (Houghton Mifflin)

Luhr, James F. (editor). *Smithsonian Earth* (DK Publishing)

Lynch, Wayne, and Aubrey Lang. *The Great Northern Kingdom: Life in the Boreal Forest* (Fitzhenry & Whiteside)

Raffan, James (editor). *Rendezvous With The Wild: The Boreal Forest* (Boston Mills)

Websites

Forest Conservation Portal **forests.org/**

Missouri Botanical Garden **mbgnet.mobot.org/**

Oregon Forest Resources Institute **www.oregonforests.org/**

Temperate Forest Foundation **www.forestinfo.org/**

University of California, Berkeley, Museum of Paleontology
     www.ucmp.berkeley.edu/glossary/gloss5/biome/forests.html

World Forestry Center **www.worldforestrycenter.org/**

WWF **www.panda.org/news_facts/education/middle_school/habitats/index.cfm**

Publisher's note to educators and parents: Our editors have carefully reviewed these Web sites to ensure that they are suitable for children. Many Web sites change frequently, however, and we cannot guarantee that a site's future contents will continue to meet our high standards of quality and educational value. Be advised that children should be closely supervised whenever they access the Internet.

Museums

American Museum of Natural History
Central Park West at 79th Street
New York, NY 10024

BC Forest Discovery Centre
2892 Drinkwater Road
Duncan, British Columbia V9L 6C2
Canada

Fisher Museum
Harvard Forest
324 North Main Street
Petersham, MA 01366

Giant Forest Museum
Sequoia National Park
California

Lusto Finnish Forestry Museum
58450 Punkaharju
Finland

National Museum of Natural History
10th Street and Constitution Avenue, NW
Washington, DC 20560-0166

Texas Forestry Museum
1905 Atkinson Drive
Lufkin, TX 75901-2505

World Forestry Center
Discovery Museum
4033 SW Canyon Road
Portland, OR 97221

GLOSSARY

broad-leaved: referring to a tree that has broad leaves (such as an oak), as opposed to needles

canopy: a forest's upper layer of leaves and branches

coniferous: cone-bearing; coniferous trees tend to have needles instead of broad leaves, and most are evergreen

deciduous: a tree or shrub that sheds its leaves during part of the year

evergreen: a tree or other plant that retains its leaves year-round

food chain: a series of organisms that depend on each other for food

fungi: a group of organisms that, like plants, tend to be fixed in one place but that, unlike plants, lack the ability to carry out photosynthesis and thus must absorb food from outside sources; mushrooms and molds are fungi

leaf litter: the layer of decaying leaves and other material on the forest floor; sometimes called leaf mold

mammals: a group of vertebrates (animals with a backbone) that nourish their young on milk produced by the mother

marsupials: a group of mammals whose young are born at an early stage of development and then continue to mature while carried in a pouch on the mother's body; most modern marsupials are found in Australasia

photosynthesis: a sunlight-based process used by geeen plants and some microorganisms to make water and carbon dioxide into food

predator: an organism that kills other organisms for food

prey: a creature killed for food by a predator

pupa: a stage in the development of certain insects, during which larvae are transformed into adults; insects in the pupal stage typically lie within a cocoon or similar protective case

resin: a sticky, generally yellow or brown substance produced by some trees and other plants for various purposes; amber is solidified ancient resin

taiga: forest of the far north, lying south of the treeless tundra; the taiga, also known as boreal (northern) forest, is dominated by coniferous trees

temperate zones: area of the Earth lying between the polar regions (located around the North and South poles) and the tropics (lying along the Equator)

tundra: a type of landscape in the polar regions featuring shrubs, mosses, plants, and the like; the ground in the tundra is permanently frozen, and trees cannot grow there

understory: the layer of a forest between the canopy and the ground layer at the forest floor; its lower part is sometimes singled out as the "shrub layer"

vegetative reproduction: a form of reproduction occurring in many types of plants in which new individuals are created without the help of seeds or spores; the new individuals may grow, for example, from extended stem structures such as runners or rhizomes or from a plant cutting that takes root

INDEX